MY SPORT
MOTORCYCLING

Tim Wood

Photographs: Chris Fairclough

Franklin Watts
London • New York • Sydney • Toronto

© 1989 Franklin Watts

Franklin Watts Inc.
387 Park Avenue South
New York
NY 10016

Phototypeset by Lineage, Watford
Printed in Italy by G. Canale & C. S.p.A. - Turin
Design: K and Co

ISBN: 0-531-10827-9
Library of Congress No: 89-50200

Illustrations: Simon Roulstone

The publishers, author and photographer
would like to thank David Heal, the Mitchell family
and Mrs. E Overend of Mallory Park Racing
Circuit for their help and cooperation in
making this book.

The motorcycle racer featured in this book is David Heal. David has always liked motor bikes. He bought a road bike as soon as he was old enough, but had a bad accident. While in hospital, he decided that it would be safer to drive a car on the road and ride bikes on race tracks. He went to Brands Hatch Racing School, in England, to learn how to race. His first serious season was in 1986, when he won four 250cc championships. In 1987, he moved up to a 350cc machine and had ninety-three victories in the season, winning the rare honor of becoming Champion of Brands Hatch. In 1988 he moved up to 750cc bikes, but his bike had mechanical problems, and he did not have the success for which he had hoped.

I am a motorcycle racer. I am racing this weekend, so I must prepare my bike. I start by propping the bike on stands and removing the faring.

The engine has been tuned by engineers, but some final adjustments to the carburetors will make sure that it is running at full power.

A racing motorcycle is a complicated piece of machinery. I need a well-equipped workshop to do repairs on my bike. I have to be my own mechanic for much of the time.

Once I have finished working on the engine, I replace the fuel tank. It slots easily into place.

When the bike is back in one piece, I load it into my van. I take a lot of spare parts, tools and several sets of racing tires with me as well.

I hitch my trailer to the van. I sleep in the
trailer during the weekend of a race meet.
It becomes my headquarters.

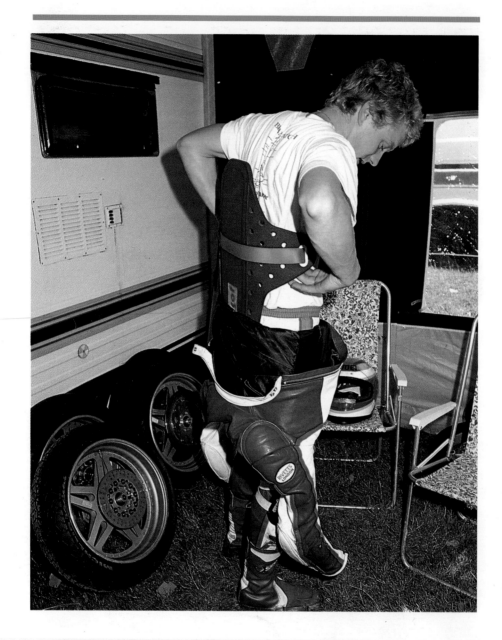

On the morning of the race, I put on my racing leathers. I strap on my back pad.

I put my chest pad in place. The leather and pads will protect me if I fall off my bike during the race. Thick plastic on my knees and boots protects my legs.

11

I take my bike to be inspected by a scrutineer. He checks it thoroughly, to make sure that it is completely safe.

Two friends, who are mechanics, drop by to see how I am. I persuade them to do some work on my bike.

More about motorcycle racing

Motorcycles race in classes according to their engine size and power. The smallest bikes have 80cc engines and the largest can be over 1300cc.

There are three main types of tires which are used in motorcycle racing. The tires used in dry conditions are called "slicks." They are completely smooth and made of a special rubber mixture that becomes sticky when hot and grips the road. They cost $160 each and can last as few as ten laps.

"Wets" are used when it is raining. Deep grooves called treads on the surface of the tires throw water away from the tires and help them grip the road.

"Intermediates" are used when the track is slightly damp. They have a small amount of tread.

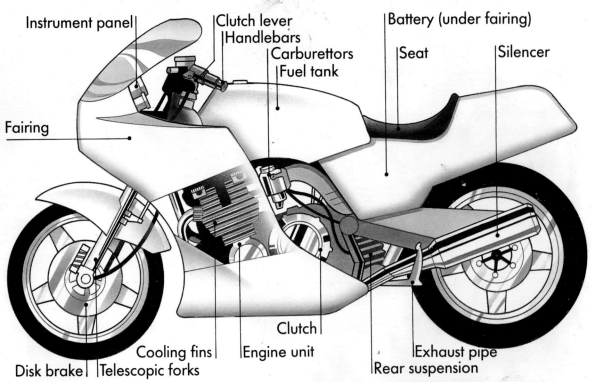

Instrument panel
Clutch lever
Handlebars
Carburettors
Fuel tank
Battery (under fairing)
Seat
Silencer
Fairing
Disk brake
Telescopic forks
Cooling fins
Engine unit
Clutch
Rear suspension
Exhaust pipe

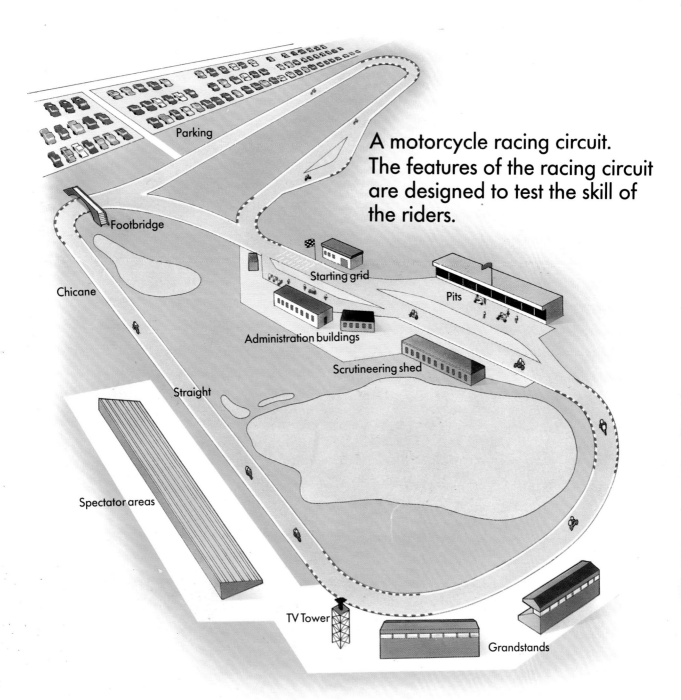

Parking

A motorcycle racing circuit.
The features of the racing circuit
are designed to test the skill of
the riders.

Footbridge

Chicane

Starting grid

Pits

Administration buildings

Scrutineering shed

Straight

Spectator areas

TV Tower

Grandstands

15

I fill the tank with fuel. The bike runs on a mixture of Avgas and gas.

I discuss my tactics for the race with my
sponsor. He is eager to see me do well, as it
will be good publicity for his company.

The race is about to start. The riders take
their places on the starting grid. The riders
in the front positions made faster lap times
in earlier practice races.

Mechanics give last-minute advice and make a few adjustments to the bikes. The riders rev their engines, waiting for the 30-second warning.

The starting light turns from red to green.
The race has begun. Some of the bikes wheelie
as they accelerate, their riders are eager
to be in front at the first corner.

A special bar keeps the handlebars from turning too far, so riders steer around corners by leaning their bikes over. Sometimes their knees touch the ground.

The riders crouch low over the handlebars to reduce their wind resistance. This helps them go faster.

I shift my weight in the saddle to help me go around this left-hand curve, which is called the Devil's Elbow.

Track marshalls use flags to signal to the riders. The green flag means that the track is clear. The riders know there is no danger ahead.

I accelerate along the straight at well over 206kph (130mph). The circuit is too small for the bike to reach its maximum speed, which is about 320kph (200mph).

Motorcycle racing can be dangerous. This rider skids coming out of a corner, slides across the track and crashes into the tire barrier. He is lucky not to be hurt.

The winner does a lap of honor, waving to the cheering crowd. Unfortunately, I do not win my race today.

After the race is over, we ride our bikes
28 back into the paddock.

All the races are over. It is time to leave the circuit. I load the bike and all my equipment back into the van.

FACTS ABOUT MOTORCYCLING

The first motorcycle was built by Gottlieb Daimler in 1885. It had a wooden frame on which was mounted a 264cc single-cylinder engine. It had a top speed of 19kph (12 mph).

The first motorcycle race was held in Richmond, England, in 1897. The race was 1.6km (1 mile) long.

The oldest motorcycle race is the Isle of Man TT. It was first held in 1907. The 60.7km (37.7 mile) circuit is also the longest used for any motorcycle race.

The highest average lap speed is 258kph (160mph) achieved by Yvon du Hamel of Canada at the Daytona International Speedway, Florida, in 1973. He was riding a 900cc Kawasaki.

The most successful motorcycle racer of all time is Giacomo Agostini of Italy. He has won fifteen World Championships.

The world speed record for a motorcycle is 513.7kph (318.6mph). This was achieved by Donald A. Vesco of the United States in 1978, on the Bonneville Salt Flats, Utah, USA. His machine, called *Lightning Bolt*, was powered by two 1016cc Kawasaki engines.

The record for the most World Championship races won in a single season is 19. It is held jointly by Giacomo Agostini of Italy and Mike Hailwood of Great Britain.

GLOSSARY

Accelerate
To make the bike go faster by twisting the accelerator which pushes more fuel into the carburetors.

Avgas
A type of fuel normally used in airplane engines.

Carburetor
Part of a gasoline engine. It mixes gas and air to create the explosive mixture needed to run the engine.

Faring
A fiberglass cover for the front of a motorcycle which allows the bike to move faster by cutting down wind resistance.

Hairpin
A very sharp turn.

Leathers
A leather suit worn by a motor bike rider.

Mechanic
Someone trained to repair and maintain motorcycles and cars.

Scrutineer
A trained mechanic whose job is to check that racing bikes are safe and have not been changed in any way that would give the rider an unfair advantage.

Sponsor
A company or individual who pays the expenses of a motorcycle racer in return for him or her advertising their products on his or her bike and clothing.

Starting grid
Rows of starting places on a racing circuit.

Index